WE WERE BORN TO DIE

A COLLECTION OF POEMS

BY

DR HARMEET KAUR BHALLA

First Published in 2021

Becomeshakespeare.com

One Point Six Technologies Pvt Ltd
123, Building J2, Shram Seva Premises, Wadala Truck Depot,
Wadala (East), Mumbai 400037, India
T: +91 8080226699

ISBN - 978-93-5458-080-2

DEDICATED TO

MY AUNT MRS VIDYAWATI KAUR

ACKNOWLEDGEMENT

Life is the most precious gift given by God. It is a sojourn wherein with each passing day, we grow and live unaware of tomorrow's happenings.

Try to be optimistic and let life take its turns. The day we accept the hard truth that we are temporary residents over here, the Universe will become free from sins.

CONTENTS

The Middle

The End

Tanka poems on LOVE

Preface

The world is a place where we are born one day and then die another day. We grow up facing the bleak realities of the world. A child is unaware of his surroundings until it gains senses. Step by step, he climbs and faces the challenges of life. He will grow up and become successful in life only if he learns the small truths of life. He grows old with all the bitter and sweet experiences of life to die one day. There is always a beginning, middle, and end of life but love holds the uppermost position because it can heal the world.

BEGINNING: The mother's lap is the most secure place for a child. The eunuchs welcome the new-born. Some places and people are gender-biased. The first lessons are learnt with parents and grandparents. The first step to a place of worship and then, to a school are taken because the values imbibed therein will remain life-long. It is actually a preparation for the future.

MIDDLE: The child grows up and is open to innumerable new happenings. At every step, he meets a variety of people. Every day is a new day. He has to choose between right and wrong. He will face challenges and even be depressed at times. The one who starts understanding the reality of life and death will stay aloof from sin. All people have to feel the presence of God.

END: The human body is made from dust and will return to dust without fail. Our body is a mere framework of bones and flesh. The soul never dies but passes on to another body. The old and bereaved wait for their last day on this earth. They cross the hurdles and reach a stage from where they will never return. They should try to pass on the message of brotherhood to the coming generations. Few are complacent, while others die with countless desires which couldn't be fulfilled in this life. The end is for all. We were born to die.

TANKA-LOVE POEMS: The Tanka is a poem of thirty-one syllables. It is a Japanese song or verse. It is a form of poem in five lines. There are five syllables in the first line, seven in the second line, five in the third, seven in the fourth and seven in the fifth 5/7/5/7/7. It has no rhyme scheme.

 My twenty-five Tanka poems are based on the way love can heal this world. It is believed that all human beings living on this earth are an amalgamation of emotions.

Above all the other factors, love holds the most prominent place. It comes in various forms and each holds a specific place. It can solve all the critical problems and give a new direction. Let us leave this world with love, love and only love.

THE BEGINNING

1.

AMALGAMATION

How many colours of dust are lying on this earth?

Everyday God picks them up as he knows it's worth

The black, brown, dusky, and white hues of dust

He makes mountains of it so that it may never rust

The elixir he pours on them to create countless moulds

Then he solemnly begins the incessant amalgamation

 Every single soul will be made into a statue of gold

Every single infant born from the womb of a mother

Will bear a non-identical façade of any one colour

Throughout their lifetime they will live with it

The blended mould will rise and mature with life

In all conditions, human beings have to stay satisfied

Outwardly your complexion will glow, inwardly your soul

The ephemeral body with the eternal soul within

Will come to an end but the soul will travel to heaven

From a mould of dust, we come down to dust again

So, let us greet our body and keep beautifying it

Keep realising the truth that, the end is dust.

2.

CREATION

The Universe swirls and twirls with his magic

We feel honoured with his extravagant creation

A combination of living and non-living beings

Every single atom and element present

Bears a stamp of his ultimate mastery

With millions and trillions of species enjoying their stay

With man above all who earns and prefers to pay

The rivers, valleys, and hills are beyond comparison

The forests, plains, and deserts look stunning

Do sit and applaud the treasures of our Lord

We are clueless of the roots of its formation

Learn to live and nurture these admirable gifts

Life runs smoothly if we balance ourselves.

3.

BIRTHING

You are floating and dancing in the womb

You wait for the birthing and want to come out soon

For nine long months, you breathed with her

For nine long months, you slept and woke up with her

For nine long months, you laughed and cried with her

For nine long months, you ate and drank with her

For nine long months every second, you grew within her

Her blood is running in your heart and veins

You have matured finally and the time is near

You are about to see sunshine, so need not fear

The excruciating pain she bears only for you

You burst out and they hold you upside down

She gives a lovely smile on hearing you cry

Your body trembles as it is out in the open now

You gently open your eyes to see the world around

Your tiny hands, feet, and fully developed body parts

She feels like a goddess and lies with you enveloped in her arms

Let your adoration for each other stay on and on.

4.

THE TINY FEET

The soft, supple, pink feet

Just the size of its mother's hand

Ten little toes with future unknown

The child moves the feet to & fro

It hits hard in the air unaware

The feet tremble when they first step down

 Tightly it holds the hands of its mother and father

They will lead the child to a zone safer

The feet are unaware of the heat and cold

They may even reach places untold

Take utmost care of your feet even when fully grown

Count your steps and reach good places that are known.

5.

THE UNKNOWN WORLD

What is the difference between a friend and foe?

The child may or may not ever know

The one who greets with a pleasant smile

Will get a quick response without waiting for awhile

The hands and feet are ready to move

They are unaware of where someone may lead

How does a snake or an elephant look?

The child may run and hold them without fear

It thinks that everything in this world is dear

What is the difference between sweet and sour?

The colours and the ripeness attract it not

It snatches the food in whichever form it comes

The immature brain of the child may hold

Very few memories once it grows old

The dreadful and hopeful reminiscences

May or may not create disturbances

Unless and until it gains the senses in proper

The unknown world will keep befooling it forever.

6.

NEW ABODE

The entrance may be in a hut or a palace

You may live and sleep on a rug or a roadside

The new abode which welcomes is the world at large

The human body blessed with inborn capacities

To try, imbibe, adjust in all circumstances

The sun for warmth, with the moon to stay cool

The trees for shelter and the air we breathe

The unmixed air to inhale and to exhale

The uncontaminated water to drink and bathe

The seasons make the stay pleasurable

The fragrance of the flowers enters the nostrils

The snow on the mountain peaks gives a chill

The Universe is full of choices for mankind at large

All these offerings of God are without any charge

Let us be gratified with these bounties large

7.

THE TRIBE

The mother is the first of the tribe

The love pours and outpours from within;

The father, though equally vital, follows

They are quite up to the mark and a bit mellow;

The tiny siblings come with a blend of emotions

Till young and innocent, they show no reactions;

The mature kinfolk differentiates between awesome and awful

The relationships may even come to a standstill;

The adoration of grandparents is always levelled

Their eyes speak of love and are unparalleled;

Consider the earth and its family fascinating

The world will become the most joyful place to live in.

8.

THE EUNUCHS REJOICE

The news is spreading like fire

The new born has arrived out of a desire

The fortunate mother enters the threshold

The infant close to her bosom she holds

Early in the morning with the sunrise

The echo of laughter with drummers from a distance

The neighbours gather to see their performance

They bang the doors and shower their blessings

In swirling motions, the eunuchs rejoice

Their caked faces with a sorrowful smile

Loaded with ornaments in satiny attires

From the mother's lap, the child silently watches them on fire

Singing and dancing in strange tones with improper steps

Then hold the child to chant their hymns

Blessings in plenty with sprinkling rice

They demand the parents a handsome price

Do not ignore or laugh your head off

They too are born as human beings

Try to give them equal respect with consideration

Their life too is full of meaning and devotion.

9.

BESTIE

The first steps to the school

The first day in the classroom

Varied looks with contrasting facades

Leaves the decent, bizarre in the class

The one sitting on the same bench

Or the other smiling from afar

Who will be my bestie?

The investigation will take time

Try to tune in with them at lunchtime

The friendship gradually sets its feet firmly and begins

The little scuffles with misunderstandings few

It hardly takes time to forget and begin anew

The foundation stone of life-long amity is laid

If true and worthy, for ages it will be portrayed.

10.

STEPS TO THE TEMPLE

The naïve child takes a leisurely walk to the temple

With his parents, he climbs the steps to the temple

He places the warm feet on the cold steps one by one

The smoke of the incense and perfume of flowers

Enter his nostrils from far and makes its home

The bells of the temple incessantly ring in his ears

The chanting of hymns by the priests in ochre clothing at large

A colourful display of idols - some standing, others sitting in a row

A coin is dropped in honour of the Lord

The hands are folded to say a solemn prayer

Free us from worries and give sincere blessings

The child gives a bizarre look to the Gods

Cool sandalwood tilak is applied on his forehead

Worried and surprised he again smiles at the Gods

Why are they motionless and mute?

The aura holy as if being welcomed by the Gods

They turn around and get down the steps

He eats the offerings and wipes his forehead.

11.

THE FIRST ALPHABET

The world is at the highest level now

As literacy holds a special place now

The child learns the language of love

Then comes the alphabet that is tough

The sleeping and the slanting lines

The horizontal and the vertical lines

The circle, square, and the rectangle

The joining of dots and colouring of pots

The rainbow of colours dancing anew

Recognition of green, black and blue

Becoming trilingual or a bilingual

Learning adaptations from formations

The recognition of the first alphabet

The earnestness remains till the last alphabet.

12.

CHILD ABUSE

The tears are streaming from their eyes

The under privileged and the orphans

Don't thrash if you find them unwise

His innocence speaks for him

He is known only to the whims

Some are tortured day and night

Few are made to stand upright

He is unknown to the good or bad world

The one who adores him becomes his world

Teach them the true meaning of love

Do not criticize to make them rough

The advantages are taken by many

They are the ones who are uncanny

They are abused, bruised and fumbled

Their immature body is trampled

They can sit in one corner and brood

Let them live with a happy mood.

13.

CHOCOLATES AND CHIPS

The attraction lies not in the greens

The taste is hardly developed till teens

When unknown to the wonderful food

The children gulp it down without objection

The colours are soon recognized

The flavours are to be taken by choice

The sweet, sour, and bitter bites

The chocolates and chips are liked

The young body is delicate and fragile

The diseases come and hinder the lifestyle

Let all parents take a sincere step

To let their child, grow and develop.

14.

DEPENDS

The voyage of life sails smoothly although

 Still, it all depends on the upbringing though

It all depends on the language you instruct

It all depends on the way you construct

It all depends on the manners you possess

It all depends on the habits that will bring success

It all depends on the differences we preach

The good or bad and hell or heaven

The right choice will take mankind

To a land of peace and prosperity though

It all depends on the way you toil

It will uplift you from the soil

The preaching and teaching should be faultless

If nothing gained life will become meaningless.

15.

BLIND FAITH

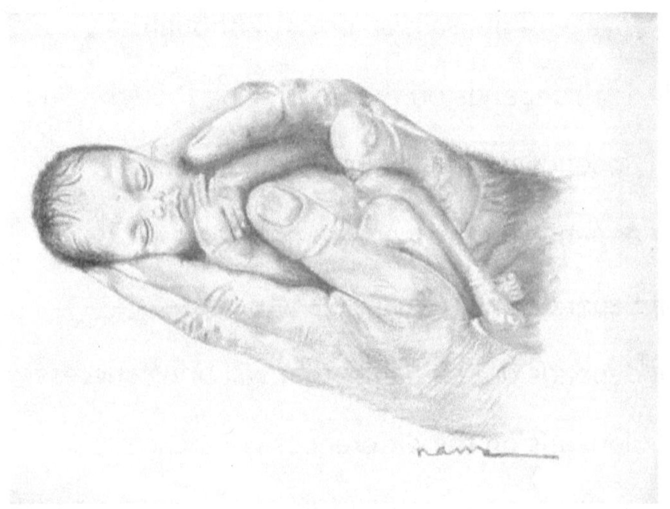

It's a girl?

Shouted the midwife at midnight

The men prepare themselves

In pitch darkness when the moon hides

With the dark clouds and the high tides

A murder of a mute and innocent

The mother's pain has not vanished

It will continue life long

The girl is wrapped in a cloth

It is carried with mouth stuffed

The grave is dug for the one alive

Are men not children of God?

The one who would have seen the world

Will breathe her last in the hands of her own

She is put silently in the grave

Her twinkling eyes are covered with mud

A woman cannot save another woman

Rise up and come forward

Take her confidently in your lap

Let her see the earth with your eyes

Save her from these early goodbyes.

16.

WHAT IS LOVE?

The meaning of love is hidden

As love comes in variations

The child is blank, knows no explanation

What is love?

Let the response be appropriate

Give it a winning definition

Mother and child need no comparison

The sibling love is at times based on conditions

In Adam and Eve, we saw

The commencement of unconditional love

It took birth in the heaven above

Some shower umpteen love

They flaunt it in the open, fearless

Others may not disclose their love

They will keep it as a silent trust

Some live and die only for love

They are the messengers of genuine love

Give your children immense love

The world will be an ecstatic place to live

If there is love, love and only love.

17.

CHILDREN

Chubby being the best creation of God

Humble with naughtiness in abundance

Imitating them all without any ego

Longevity is what everyone wishes for

Delighted at every action along with reaction

Righteousness is prominent

Expressiveness is lacking behind

Naive with an unsophisticated mind

18.

HE OR SHE

The birth is always a surprise

Either he or she will arrive

Both the genders are precious

They are present with the same conscious

He may receive greater affection

He may enjoy and live with relaxation

He is considered to continue the generation

He has to live up to everybody's expectations

She is an angel from heaven

She will have to live with restrictions

She will be submissive and full of patience

She will be responsible for the coming generations

Let us eliminate gender disparities

Let us be content with a he or she

They are incomplete without each other

Let them carve a niche for one another.

19.

AMUSEMENT

The soft and gentle brain is silent but chuckles

Till it starts noticing the things happening around

The mischievousness lies in the two small eyes

It struggles for freedom and to move around

The giggling and laughter with thin lips and tiny teeth

The colourful dolls and animals

The rainbow- coloured blocks and houses

The superfast fancy toy cars and lorries

They build an amusement park of their own

The look into the mirror with strange expressions

Their life is not based on any conditions

It is always a curious world in which they live

Let childhood be pleasurable so let them thrive.

20.

SHARING

Moral habits taught when young

Will forever make us sing an ecstatic song

We are born with a materialistic notion

Unless we are taught to share our portion

Some have too much, some too little

The art of sharing lies in the middle

If we teach every human to look at the down-trodden

None of them will ever sleep hungry or eat rotten

Sharing always gives immense satisfaction

Share good thoughts, etiquettes and virtues

Sharing and caring should be followed by all; not few.

21.

CHILD LABOUR

Why am I not rich like other children?

The question remains unanswered for many

The world is a place where you strive

You toil day and night in order to thrive

Every parent wants the best for his child

He makes both ends meet in order to survive

The poor child looks up at other affluent ones

His small hand and feet should hold a pencil or pen

The circumstances make him work from eight to ten

The burden he carries strains his soft muscles

The clean hands and feet are completely blackened

Let all parents give equal rights to children

Let them breathe fresh air in the open

Let them study the alphabets and become literate

Put an end to child labour and be considerate.

22.

DREAMLAND

It is believed that children remember their previous birth

They live in a dreamland until they gain senses on this earth

They chuckle on the mere thought of their happy moments

They cry at the horrendous memories of their tragic moments

The child is completely free from the responsibilities plenty

As it is ignorant to the relationships and duties aplenty

The world is the most mesmeric and authentic place

Unless and until it starts understanding its worth

These dreams slowly lose vitality and come to an end

On the day one grows up and fails to pretend.

23.

THE CRADLE

The bells of the orphanage keep ringing

The cries of children keep on mingling

The cradle lies covered in the open

Welcoming the infant who is God's creation

Let your love be pure and serene

Let not relationships be left unseen

For these mistakes of their life

The unborn have to pay for it a price

The child who was their flesh and blood

Becomes an illegitimate as it enters the world

If by chance the fault is known in time

Do comprehend your terms in the prime

The child will live with complications plenty

 Throughout the life its demands will be scanty

In every parent he will search for his own

So, let us try to give him a home of his own.

24.

FESTIVALS

A land of varied colours and religions it is

My country is grounded with cultures and showbiz

Throughout the year the festivals galore

They leave a message of brotherhood to the core

January enters with the chilly winds

The beginning of a new year with bliss

The burning of fire, dance and music on Lohri

Pongal and the holy festival of Makar Sankranti

February comes with the passionate winter

The kites soaring high on Basant Panchami

The auspicious yellow flowers and saffron food

People glide gaily in their yellow dresses openly

March is the most awaited month full of colours

The Holika Dahan or bonfire and victory of good over evil

The powdered, liquid and naturally made herbal hues

The relishing of sweetmeats with the birth of Lord Shiva

April is the month of fun and frolic

Vaisakhi comes with the birth of New Solar Year

It comes with the birth of Khalsa

Purifying ourselves with elixir by being baptised

The winter months commence with Dussehra

The killing of Ravana symbolises victory of good over evil

The return of the Lord Rama, Laxman and Sita after fourteen years exile

With the festival of lights, we celebrate Diwali

With the chilly winds and snow-covered houses

On December 25th we celebrate Christmas with the birth of Jesus Christ

When Santa Claus comes singing on the sledge

He takes the children to a happy and sensational world.

25.

BEGINNING

Birth is a blessing for every human being

Earth welcomes all to a land of surprises

Generations will keep moving on and on

Identify yourself with utmost sincerity

Numerous ideologies will be forced

Nurture your thoughts by choosing right

Ideal person you have to become

Noble work will lead to success

Greatness lies in having a good beginning

THE MIDDLE

26.

SINCERE GROWTH

The timidness with playfulness comes to a halt

The body which we admire to the fullest

Suddenly takes a serious separate turn

A girl or boy feel the body inside out

They look at themselves from top to bottom

They scrutinize themselves from left to right

The swelling of a few areas leaves them surprised

Sincere growths at places leaves them galvanized

The mirror becomes the most trusted friend

The number of times will you gaze at it unflinchingly no one knows

At times a fit of rage, while on others a gladdened surprise

A blend of emotions rising from the innermost depth

Growing of the mind with the body growth

Will give confidence and fragrance of rose.

27.

THE CRACK OF DAWN

Every morn we wake up to surprises

We open our eyes as the sun rises

We stretch ourselves at the crack of dawn

The cock crows and welcomes the dawn

We feel gently the fresh morning breeze

We smile on seeing the butterflies fluttering their wings

The twittering of sparrows on guava trees

The ears listen to the buzzing of the bees

It wakes us up, makes us complete

 The dewy morning incense we inhale

With morning tea, we sit and relax

We start training our mind for the day

We chalk out plans for the entire day

Meetings, sessions, and the daily chores

Will be outlined according to minutes and hours

This is the human design for next twenty-four hours

The plan of God is set and above all

He never discloses the happenings of minutes and hours.

28.

I AM GOD

The youth today is adamant and aggressive

They find only themselves impressive

Unfamiliar to the difference between ebb and flow

Unknown to the difference between fast and slow

Unexplored lies still the settings high and low

Undistinguished are the reasons of mirth and sorrow

The mind seems to have crossed all stages of maturity

They themselves are the only priority

If ever questioned about the existence of the Almighty

To a few notorious ones living lively

I am God, I am superior to all

Is the only response coming from all

A day comes when you bow down at the altar

You will recognize the space he has created

For you are his bright radiating star.

29.

THE ART TO LISTEN

I'm tired of the ongoing commotion

There is no silence now; only motion

The two ears placed on the face

Balances and gives a special grace

They imbibe the voice deep within

Help it to reach straight up to the pinnacle

Some voices may be strong which hurt

They break the still and silent path

Some voices may be good to hear

They leave you without any fear

Some voices may be judgemental

They will never let you crumble

Some are voices of the egoist

They may hinder you the greatest

Some are the voices of leaders

They may at times make you stronger

Some are the silent voices of love

They will lead you to promises of happiness

The greatest quality for an efficient journey of life

Is the art to listen and let the good things happen.

30.

CONFIDENCE

Capable of doing the impossible

Opportunities come in great numbers

Noble in deeds and profession

Fabulous will be the outcome

Impeccable will be the goal to be

Dynamic you have to become

Enlightened by the holy path

Numerous hurdles you have to cross

Charming personality builds confidence

Energetic physique gives utmost strength

31.

Birds and Animals

The unspeakable creatures of earth

Born they are with the same worth

The deep-coloured birds fly

In the blue sky low and high

They search for food and water

They have no foundations

The eagles, vultures and falcons

The swans, parrots and sparrows

They assemble their own nest

For them it is the best

No troubles and conditions are set

Let humans play a vital role in their life

Serve them grains and water daily

Let them glide in the sky gaily

The animals loiter around smoothly

They live a life empty, disconnected blindly

From early morning to horrendous night,

 In sunshine and dreamy moonlight

They live fearless, with humans being as masters

Some get a home as they are tamed to give joy

The forest is a secretive place for the man-eating ones

The poisonous reptiles may even kill man

The Lion being the King of the Jungle

Does not allow anyone to mingle

Let them relax in the dense jungles

Don't let their life be entangled.

32.

CURIOSITY

Candid you are though you may dilly-dally

Utilize your intelligence in the best possible way

Radical change may take place

Ideas keep cropping in your mind

Outcome should be healthy

Soul may retain its purity

Instantaneous results are wanted

Tactfulness may lead to positive results

Yearning for the best

33.

GREEN AND CLEAN

Millions of years back the land was full of nature's grace

Rivers, streams and springs of clear water did flow at a slow pace

The mountains, hills and valleys gave a mesmerising glow

The deserts breathed with sand dunes and an oasis though

The grasslands and the plains glistened with fresh dewdrops

The earth was bearable as it was neither too hot nor too cold

The volcanoes remained dormant and the lava kept boiling

Humans built houses and huts with nature's products although

Humanity lived merrily with meagre belongings in their abode

The millions of years have crossed with lack of nature's grace now

Rivers, streams and springs of polluted water flow with a great speed

The mountains, hills and valleys stand aloof with tainted frigidity

The deserts lie dry, parched, waterless where the sandstorms blow

The earth is now unbearable where the blazing sun shines and chilly wind blow

The volcanoes have brought death and destruction with the hot lava flow

The cemented, bricked and marble houses have blocked the way

Humanity is estranged with plenty of possessions lying scattered.

34.

ENTERTAINMENT

The young, old and diseased

Need some leisure to please

Twenty-four hours in a single day

 You begin your day with prayer

The daily chores everyday keep you engaged

Your intense work for survival keeps you caged

Too much of exertion leaves you perplexed

Is this your life, free from entertainment and rest?

The monotony of life gets on the nerves

Every single soul looks for mirth, not unhappiness

The mind and body need to be rejuvenated

You can either take a nap or go for a walk

You can either go for a pilgrimage or a hill top

You can play indoor and outdoor games

You can read or write as you please

You can gossip or listen to preaching

You can relax in your beautiful house

Pass your time with his presence by your side.

35.

DEFINITION OF HAPPINESS

What is the secret of happiness?

A question was asked to God calmly

The secret lies within you, child

He answered with a smile

Let the mind take decisions

Face good things with generosity

The journey of life is full of vicissitudes

You may either rise or even fall

You may face a storm or gentle snowfall

It is better to feel the essence of life

It is gifted only once not twice

Try to bear the pains with a smile

It would then become so easy to pass your life.

36.

ADDICTION

Alcohol is spreading its roots in young

Drugs have poisoned the veins of some

Daring and the handsome young

Injecting themselves and displaying strength

Corruption is everywhere on the rise

Tarry no one needs surprise

Intoxicating and considering a status symbol

One by one diseases crop in

Nation is dying; stop addictions of all kind

37.

SENSATIONS

Every growing body has sensations

Every growing guy and girl have botheration

The opposite sex always attracts

Choices are innumerable, a few apt

Impressions seem to be intact

New love bends and straightens

The entire Universe looks like a land of love

The heart pounds faster and faster

On seeing a brown, black or white

Love is blind - it is believed in history

Your closeness increases with the passage of time

 You exchange glances whenever you get time

Some take for granted, others wholehearted

Some pursue for months, others lifelong

If sincere carry on; otherwise, hold back strongly

Life and time are precious so manage boldly

38.

WHO WILL SUCCEED?

It is a rat race

Where all live in their space

They are trying their best

To stand out from the rest

Hard labour and devotion

Brings loads of success

But still the question arises

Who will succeed?

In this ultra-modern world

Very few are grounded

Stuck to their roots

Infinite choices lay bare

Choose the one for which you care

If laborious and diligent you are

Then success is not far

If honesty is running in your blood

Then you will bloom to a flower from a bud

All humans are rated differently

They will earn accordingly

Be content and fortunate with your riches

It is a blessing of Almighty who always watches.

39.

HIDE AND SEEK

At times we want to shut ourselves

In the dark well away from our own self

When the humiliation becomes unbearable

The task is at times still incomplete

A person close to you may leave

Your countless passions lie defeated

We wait for sunshine from dusk to dawn

For a radiant morn to come along

We strive to succeed in our goals

We bear the grunts and rise up

We try to live up and never give up

We find ourselves in the game of hide and seek.

40.

DESTINATIONS

Dreamy lands are in abundance

Eastern and Western horizons

Southern and Northern hemispheres

Travel you can to favourite destinations

Ice cold glaciers and lands are welcoming

North Pole and the South Pole are far apart

Arctic and Atlantic blue oceans

Tirelessly stretching to faraway lands

Indian Ocean stands aloof

Ostentatious display of artificial buildings

No man's land too we can reach

41.

I AM THE BEST

No one can survive with this epithet

That in this world I am the best

The dogma is set by the society

It is contrasting in every country

Every individual is independent

To give a trial to something new

Failures and successes depend on hard work

Hard work is the pillar to success

It may take ages to reach the top

Unless you don't want to stop

Try, try, and you will succeed

Your experiences you can preach

Every occurrence leaves with you a lesson

With these your thoughts always broaden

Don't sit back and cry over spilled milk

There are still destinations you have to reach.

42.

IN VOGUE

Leading the crowd is a dream

The adolescent lads and lasses

Love to dress in their favourite attire

Everyone has a desire to be seen

The silks, satins, muslins and linens

In blues, oranges, pinks and purples

They keep themselves updated to see

 What is in vogue?

Wear a garment which suits your body

Drape yourself in your darling colours

The four seasons are to be kept in mind

The snowfall, rain and the sunshine

Don't spend too many dollars and coins

Some have scanty others superfluous

There are many living bald and bare

Lying out in cold and heat exposed

Cover them up with clothes of tenderness

Let them also wear their choicest dresses.

43.

LEARN TO SAY NO

In the class you are taught about variations

The sun is hot while the moon is cool

Their lies a contrast between ugly and beautiful

The greatness lies in the essence of the soul

The guiltless, placid and the white soul

Will soon turn guilty, sooty as a charcoal

If they never learn to say no

Say no if someone forces to tell lies

Say no if someone compels to commit a crime

Say no if someone asks to disrespect elders

Say no if someone asks to dishonour the girl child

Say no if someone asks to befool parents

Say no if someone asks to be intolerant

Say no if someone wants you to become an atheist

These refusals will build your inner strength

It is better to keep negative people at arm's length.

These refusals will build your inner strength

It is better to keep negative people at arm's length.

44.

MY VALENTINE

We are unknown to the essence of love

Till our heart starts beating for someone

Our eyes are always searching for the one

The one who will be the best among several who blossom

The question can be put forward gently

Will you be my Valentine?

If the Lord above wishes wholeheartedly

The Sun, Moon, and stars shine from above

To decipher the true meaning of love

The answer will be given patiently

Destiny brings the people who love together

A stranger suddenly becomes a lover

All the hurdles will now be crossed together

On the lifeboat they will sail together

They will create a home full of love

The answer is given to the Lord above.

45.

JUNK

The brain and the body will soon junk

If unnecessary things in it are sunk

Try to make it a storehouse of knowledge

Try to fill it with unconditional love

Try to load it with exuberance aplenty

Try to maintain your self-dignity

Try to keep yourself forever alive

Try to maintain a healthy lifestyle

Try to get in nutrition's compulsory

Try to derive pleasure from the music of choice

Try to relax your body and mind with a sweet voice

Try to keep exasperation at a distance

Try to remember God and feel the existence.

46.

ROAD TO SUCCESS

The road to success is full of potholes

We fall and get injured

We start losing ourselves in and out

We think we are failures at last

The road will never be smooth

People will try to disapprove

The essence lies in becoming exceptional

Like a phoenix you rise gloriously

Let the bygones be bygones

Let the future take its turn

It may be a rebirth

A rejuvenation you desired

Failures are the pillars to success

A glorified person you become

Magnificent is your outcome

Impossible heights you may achieve

There is no need to retreat.

47.

EXPOSURE

We flaunt our figure from the day we flourish

Some try to envelope themselves from head to toe

Some expose their body and let it go

The graceful treasured human body

Try to maintain its virginity

The masculine and the feminine

The purity and impurity lie in the mind

The human hearts keep beating

A few with eyes hovering

A few with mouth watering

A few with lips smacking

The spotless will be besmirched

The body will become corrupted

This sin will go lifelong

Don't lose yourself so easily

Be courageous and pass life gaily

The choice of securing our body belongs to us

We should never try to create a buzz

Exposure may at times lead to devastation

Think and try to be pious and strong.

48.

PROCREATION

The need to run the planet is necessary

The circle of life moving is compulsory

Man and woman were the first creations

Heaven itself favoured them in procreation

The child born from the mother's womb

Will carry their name later or soon

Every living creature on this earth

Has the right and duty to give birth

The humans carry it with sincerity

While animals are mindless with insincerity

Do give a home to the one born to a mother

Don't leave it abandoned in the hands of another.

49.

MARRIAGE - ARRANGED TO LOVE

Marriages are made in heaven it is believed

In a lifelong affinity gracefully, it is weaved

A man and a woman are brought together

They are given a task to endeavour

Each day comes with a fresh start

You comprehend each other with full heart

The views may never match at times

Try to make adjustments at difficult times

No two people born on this earth are similar

By letting each other down you may not become greater

Love blossoms and you become compatible

You start considering each other honourable

Arranged marriages lead to love definitely

When your joys and sorrows become one naturally

The day arrives when you become best friends

You gain each other's confidence.

50.

MIDDLE

Meaningless or meaningful life will become

Ideologies we have to sum

Disagreement at certain opinions

Doubtful at certain serious up comings

Lustre and wealth steal the show

Examination is still slow

THE END

51.

WHAT IS SOUL?

The body is what we admire

We cover the scars got without desire

Some parts covered, some open though

We walk and run with the flow

The figure keeps growing with the years

None of them know how it grows

Something is lying unseen, untold

What is soul?

Since childhood we have overheard

The tales told by the ones who grow old

Do your best till the last day on earth

As your soul will fly from the body for rebirth

It will not be visible to naked eyes

The carcass will lie still and passive

The soul rises above and takes a flight

The heaven will welcome the ones who do right

Hell will greet the souls of those who backbite

The pure soul is transparent, as white as snow

So, from the depth feel our soul and let it always glow.

52.

THE SICK FRAMEWORK

The life passed was with milk and roses

Neither a single body part ached nor twisted

The heat and cold was bearable by all

The hardest eatables were digestible

The softest ones made one flexible

The beautiful body that looked mystical

May turn in to something tragical

No one wants diseases in plenty

The heart, liver, kidney and stomach

They pump and let you live an epoch

The decay begins with the passage of time

The naked eyes that admired the world

May lose their shine and even turn blind

The limbs and muscles which depict their strength

May become feeble and less in length

Be prepared for the worst may happen

Turn to the Lord from the beginning

Try to leave the world without sinning

Otherwise, the body which you forever adored

May be left as a sick framework.

53.

THE SPIRITUAL JOURNEY

The smooth flow of the river

On the pious banks of Mandakini river

Reminds us of blessed Sita

The barefooted Lord Ram, Laxman and Sita

Making their lives in the forest

The dense jungles of Chitrakoot

The obedient son and brother

Left their home in Ayodhya

Life taught them to be a fighter

Bear all the pains with patience

You have given a lesson to the coming generations

There is nothing difficult in this world

Let not greatness block your path

Always face the struggles and give a fresh start.

54.

MISTAKES OF LIFE

We look to the left and then the right

We want our soul to be clean and bright

Did we ever care for the mistakes of our life?

If ever there was a proposal for committing sin

Only a hundred out of thousand thought not to win

If there was a proposal to hide the truth and tell a lie

Only a hundred out of thousand didn't want to cry

If there was a proposal to be a flirt and to show infidelity

Only a hundred in a thousand believed in fidelity

If there was a proposal to disrespect elders

Only a hundred out of thousand didn't let their life plunder

If there was a proposal to steal something precious

Only a hundred out of thousand considered it dangerous

The world wants thousand out of thousand to follow

That the Lord above watches; so, don't make your life hollow.

55.

TRANQUILITY

Transparent are the thoughts till immature

Racing on an endless path

Artistic is his creativity

Noble are his thoughts

Quietly we exit this world

Untimely or timely we may leave

Indecent to decent approvals

Life had given endless options

Identify yourself from first to last

Travel we will to an unknown sphere

Young, old and children all will leave

56.

LIFE-EXPERIENCES

Every little error with every serious mistake

Every step taken may either be careful or carefree

At times you may reach an ethereal world of ecstasy

Sometimes you may fall in a deep pit with no mercy

Each day the sun rises with new experiences of life

The strange universe with crowds of people

With whom you will start your day, nobody knows

With whom you will end your day, nobody knows

The journey from childhood to adult to old age

Some words are spoken, others left unspoken

The blissful experiences teach us life is the gift of God

The tragic experiences teach that experiments are done
by God

The ones you grow up with may leave you some day

The ones surrounding you may change their way

Every experience always leaves us with a lesson

That the humans of this world are a combination.

The tragic experiences teach that experiments are done
by God

57.

UNFINISHED

The time is less and work to be done is more

There are day dreams with which we live off and on

The desires take various shapes in contrasting forms

The tasks given are at times bearable

They are close to the heart and interesting

At times the, chores are unbearable

The ones for which there are mood swings are uninteresting

The ones that are close to our heart will be finished

By hook or by crook they will be accomplished

The deliberately thrusted will be left unaccomplished

The end of life is surprising without any disclosure

Sincere habits are those when you do your duty timely

There are humans who are indolent waiting for another day

The successful ones complete their piece of work on the same day.

58.

SURVIVED

We have sailed through the flooded river and survived

The end is near now the memories gently flash

We are thankful to God for pulling and pulling

At places when the situation became uncontrollable

The stones were hurting we were barefooted

Red blood was dripping from our tender feet

The intense pain was gripping the entire body

We had a heart to endure the sufferings

We had tears in the eyes to drop them if unfortunate

We had ears to listen and ignore the criticisms

We had a mind to think less to keep away from depression

We created our own space free from enviousness and rage

This was the only practice left to survive

You came and held me with a beautiful surprise.

59.

TILL DEATH DO US PART

The day I saw you my heart went thud

I never knew the true meaning of love

Your ocean eyes met the downcast eyes of mine

From that very moment I knew you were mine

We decided to create a world of our own

Where seeds of love and companionship will be sown

Our views didn't match but we adjusted

Our sincere thoughts for each other lasted

Passions outgrew and love blossomed

To each other we soon became accustomed

Sharing and caring and loads of adoration

I was blessed with extraordinary affection

 Life will never be same like a bunch of roses

They will fade and lose their fragrance

I know one may have to leave the other

Very few partners leave the world together

The mystery of departing is full of terror

It is difficult to live without one another.

60.

ISOLATION

Innumerable thoughts occupy the mind

Suffocation is brought forward by negative notions

Opportunities lie at every step

Lamentable becomes the condition at times

Adjustments are required at times

Transforming yourselves is the remedy

Ideological strategies will be applied

Optimism removes loneliness

Never give up believe in togetherness

61.

THE THIRD EYE

Placed on the forehead in the middle

An eye half open magnanimous and large

The two eyes speak a different story

The third eye keeps the world balanced at large

Sitting on the snow-capped mountain

With the snake encircling your neck

Daring, dashing with your life-partner sitting beside

Your farsightedness holds you back

Your worshippers' throng at the temple

To bathe you with milk and cover with ashes

You can move mountains and bring the storm

You can melt the glaciers, and cause floods

The third eye of Lord Shiva will shake the world

If ever the Lord tries to open, it will destroy the world.

62.

OUR THOUGHTS

Our thoughts mature with the growing years

They dance and sing in the beginning years

No fear of losing or winning is in the mind

We close our eyes to certain things as if we are blind

We are unknown to the true meaning of love

Love conquers and hate subsides

Then our thoughts gain maturity with us

We gain insight and welcome God

He becomes our mentor and guide

He is the one who rules our thoughts

Then we are at ease now and forever

He makes us laugh and rarely cry

We start living and loving life forever and ever.

63.

SWEET AND SOUR

What relationships will we leave behind?

With the people coming from sources combined

A few will leave you surprises many

They are a blend of characters plenty

A few are the genuine ones

With whom we develop relationships sublime

A few are the comic ones

The humour in them creates atmosphere healthy

A few are there with a tender heart

Their doting leaves a special mark

A few are the callous ones

Their harsh attitudes leave a scar

A few are the bright intellectuals

They try to learn and maintain their level

A few are the prompt and proper

They always make their lives super

Every person is born with a new temperament

Some are silent while others loquacious

Some create disturbances while others bring depression

No need to give deep thoughts to the ones useless

There are many who make lives mysterious

Live with the reality that you are the withering flower

Keep in mind that relationships may be sweet and sour.

64.

THE MAGICAL FLUTE

I often wake up with the mesmerising sound

When I hear the flute of my Lord playing around

My body shivers and my feet start moving

I gain courage and my eyes are wide open

I stand blank faced with no one around

But I can feel his presence all around

Then strange things start happening suddenly

Mystical and magical experience I have gradually

The shadow of my Lord stands with me

I am content, complete and grateful

He is standing with me through thick and thin

He frees the world from worries and sin

He only needs you to remember him

So let us make the world the best place to live in.

65.

THE HOLY GANGA

The ice- cold water from Gangotri

Pious, pure and crystal clear

A duty it fulfils on this earth

Will human ever know its worth?

Rushing and gushing among mountains

Reaching obediently to the plains

Then gradually blue turns brown

Dragging the silt, weeds

Whatever comes on the way

The hue from brown to black

From purity to impurity

The mankind becomes contaminated

Now it cannot be rated

The elixir that touched the soul

Is now present with an unsafe goal

I love to watch the flowing Ganga

Satisfying the people on the plains

My holiness remains intact

It quenches my thirst always

Let it remain magnanimous and calm

Then it will save you from all harm

Let us take a pledge everyday

Save the rivers tomorrow and today.

66.

SILENT EYES

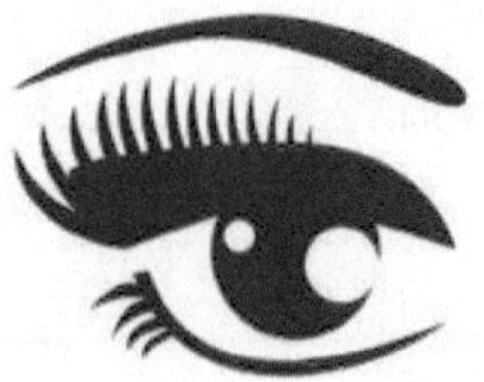

Somethings disclosed something lacking

Still waiting still memorizing

A twist and turn it often takes

Lying embedded and calm

Carrying loads of charm

A thought process of decades

The unspoken silent eyes of humans

Loaded with tears of happiness and sorrow

Every day they open up wide

By the grace of the Lord

To a bright and sunny morn

We watch his magical creation

Let us not be ignorant and blind

Let us wipe the tears of the diseased

Let us be charitable to the needy

Let us leave our eyes for someone

The one who can fathom the world

Enjoy the beauties of this Universe

That are graceful and wholesome.

67.

THE FINAL CALL

It will be silently whispered in your ears

There won't be anyone shrieking from afar

The winds will blow in the direction leading to you

The words coming out will speak only to you

The invisible, unseen force will come to take you

The one going will only notice a shadow coming

Speechless he will become on the arrival

A quiet look to the ones standing and sitting

Don't be afraid as he sent you on this earth

The patience lies in realizing the worth

They will be the ones who will be missing

You will now travel to another world

Where you will lose your memory

You will now live with another story.

68.

SOJOURN

On the lone sea-shore we stand aloof

There is no need to give a proof

We cannot count the minutes and seconds

For God wanted us to be genuinely present

The birth from a mother's womb was the beginning

This sojourn will always have a surprise ending

We were running, running and running

We were unaware whether we were losing or gaining

We broke and made several relationships

We spoke many lies to gain friendships

Now worn out and spiritless we wait

The tasks will be counted from date

In the next life the only saviour will be God

He has made two roads one narrow, the other broad

They lead to the underworld beyond the sea-shore

No one knows who will gain the highest score

69.

WE WERE BORN TO DIE

I came to this world with a loud cry

Till then I never knew the actuality

We were born to die

I grew up in the shadow of my parents

I was not open to all but shy

We were born to die

I started exploring the vast world

I came across the meaning of you and I

We were born to die

I met several new faces

Some entered my life never to say goodbye

We were born to die

The relationships soared high

In the long run a few became dry

We were born to die

I toiled day and night

Hard and fast rules I did apply

We were born to die

I welcomed the old age

I could never live in a cage but wanted to fly

We were born to die

Someone was following me

Someone wanted to live with me and die

We were born to die.

The heaven and hell are welcoming

The soul will leave without any reply

We were born to die.

70.

SUSPENSE

Silently death approaches every human body

Untimely or timely you have to accept

Surrender to the Lord completely

Plausible it is in reality

Entrance depends on your deeds

Narrating the story of virtue and vice

Superpower will greet you warmly

Exit your soul from the body

71.

I CAN SEE YOU COMING

The wait is over now

I can see you coming

In the dense fog

From one end of the road

The fog lifts slowly

I stand erect and straight

I look on both the sides and behind

I want to go alone

I know no one will accompany

My hands are empty

I was born empty-handed

Then why did I gather

Hundreds of useless items

He is like a shadow calling me

He stretches his hands

I slowly move forward

I can hear the wailing

Some loved me truly

Others were fake

They had a smile beneath

Children, grandchildren life partner

Gather around the corpse

 I am now holding his hand

I can witness myself dead.

72.

THE DIVINE CALL

There is no need to stand in a queue

He gives a call when he is valued

We search for him, in woods and mountains

He is present in the winds and the rains

He is present in every living being

He is the magnetic force present on earth

If you remember him with a true heart

Miracles start happening forgetting the past

We are his children from birth till death

We bow our head to him to be blessed

We know you will never leave us depressed

You are paving a new path we are honoured.

73.

WILL MEET YOU IN HEAVEN

How much I love you nobody knows

My sensual belief day by day grows

My day starts with your pleasant smile

My day ends looking at your graceful eyes

You are my sunshine and star

I want you near and never far

I never knew the true meaning of love

Until I got to know you as such

In times of distress, you stand by me

You never let me fall but hold me tight

My love for you forever overflows

From deep down my heart, it pours

The term death haunts me day and night

Who will be the one left in plight?

If one of us leaves don't go in depression

I promise I will surely meet you in heaven.

74.

LEAVE YOUR NAME

From dust to dust you will become

No matter how many obstacles you overcome

In the frame you will hang in one room

With a garland of roses and sandalwood soon

A few generations will remember you

Your works may have gained popularity though

The house where you lived is by your name

The children you have bear your name

Your clothes and belongings bear your name

You made a signature of your name

Your name is known in your surroundings

Some talk about praiseworthy aspects, others shortcomings

Leave your name in such a manner

That your successors live under your banner

The ones who leave a mark are remembered

The names of rest are simply shattered.

75.

END

Entrance leads to an exit

Night and day become one

Death is the final call for all

TANKA POEMS
ON
LOVE

76.

HEALING

Do not cry alone

love will heal you thoroughly

there will be fever

but it will soon subside

you will come out shining bright

77.

SUFFOCATION

Behind the closed doors

something hurts I am alone

take me to my love

suffocation is filling me

there is no fresh air to breathe

78.

REFLECTION

In you I often see

my reflection though

I admire you with sincerity

so that you may always shine

and may love reflect our thoughts.

79.

WAITING

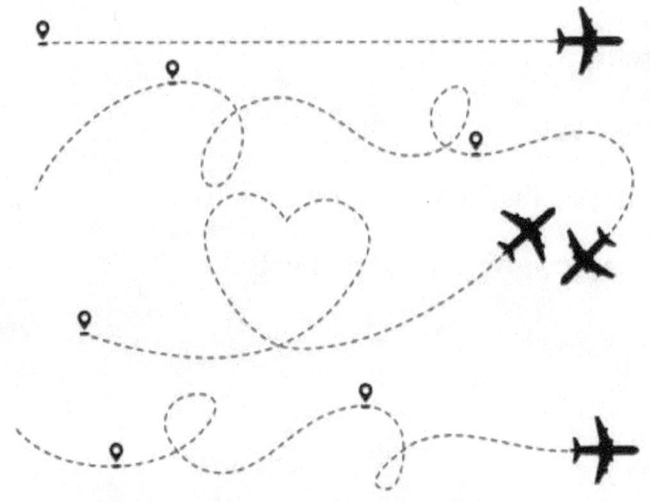

We are miles apart

our hearts are still connected though

I stand at the door

my eyes are tired and hungry

I am still waiting for you.

80.

PASSIONATE

My love for you will

grow every single moment

let me devour it

up above the horizon

let the sky speak my story.

81.

DECEPTIVE

You love many I know

let there be no mask at all

in my love at last

don't play hide and seek with me

let your love not be deceptive.

82.

CRUEL

The cruelty in love is

hitting and suffocating

no one knew you are so harsh

the scars are fresh and still there

my heart aches and it still bleeds.

83.

MAKING LOVE

Come and hold me tight

you touch my cold and dull body

I melt in your arms

then I dazzle top to toe

love will continue till end.

84.

BROKEN

Spurned and bitten in love

eyes swollen with body aching

my tears have dried now

depressed on an endless road

I stand broken forever.

85.

DEAD

When love is found dead

it shines like a star up bright

up above very far

the days pass like centuries

there are so many boundaries.

86.

PAST

Love stories of past

unforgettable at last

they creep in slowly

to find a place in the heart

better forget them at last.

87.

DISTANCES

We are far, far away

there is no certainty now

when two of us meet

don't make me ever cry aloud

for I know you will come soon.

88.

UNSPOKEN

I am now speechless

as the words of love are stuck

an unspoken love

I don't want it to die hidden

as my last breath speaks of love

89.

DELIBERATE

Oh, love for you please

will never have place in my heart

as it is considered false

it can never ever be forced if

it is a deliberate.

90.

ONE-SIDED

This one-sided love

gives more pain than pleasure

it is out of reach

sometimes it may take many years

to leave a silent message.

91.

MILLIONAIRE

I don't have diamonds

I am not a millionaire

but my love is rich

and it should not be counted

in pennies, rupees and dollars.

92.

ILLICIT

Is there purity

or is there a deep-meaning

in the art of love

illicit love is harmful

it is due to seduction.

93.

TRUE-LOVE

True love lives forever

only death separates it

though it still depends

on this earth the two may meet

or not but feelings are deep.

94.

CASTEISM

All are born equal

love does not speak of any caste

they believe in love

only endless fights take place in

casteism is not accepted.

95.

SURVIVAL

Love will rise and fall

from all sides if it requires

in its survival

then it grows slowly and gains

confidence for existence.

96.

SIBLING

Born from the same womb

let your love grow everyday as

the same blood runs in

our veins so let distances never

obstruct as sibling love grows.

97.

PARENTAL LOVE

This unending love

has no if and but

because it happens

first to last parental love

you nurtured for nine long months.

98.

FRIEND

Who to look up to?

In times of distress, it is

always a true friend

who will sit and listen to me,

in happiness and sadness.

99.

LOVE FOR GOD

In my love for God

I never calculate it

the birth and then want of death

then leads to the final call

no boundaries are required.

100.

Love Will Save the World

Unending wars

passions, likings never die

unspeakable love

one day love will heal the world

and then one day save the world.

www.ingramcontent.com/pod-product-compliance
Lightning Source LLC
LaVergne TN
LVHW091708190726
843493LV00001B/199